Classic

BIKES

A collection of iconic & much-loved classics

Mason Crest

Contents

2

Mason Crest
450 Parkway Drive, Suite D
Broomall, PA 19008
www.masoncrest.com

MAR 0 1 2016

©2016 by Mason Crest, an imprint of National Highlights, Inc.

Printed and bound in the United States of America.

10 9 8 7 6 5 4 3 2 1

Cataloging-in-Publication Data on file with the Library of Congress.

Series ISBN: 978-1-4222-3275-0
Hardback ISBN: 978-1-4222-3277-4
ebook ISBN: 978-1-4222-8515-2

Written by: Devon Bailey

Images courtesy of Shutterstock and Wiki Commons

Ariel Square Four

The Ariel Square Four was produced for 25 years in a range of 500cc to 1000cc models. The Square Four had been designed by Edward Turner who drew his original idea for the motorcycle on the back of a cigarette packet. After taking it to several manufacturers, Ariel was willing to develop Turner's design and put it into production. Turner was hoping to install a four-cylinder engine that was small enough for use in a solo motorcycle, but could produce enough power for really high performance.

When introduced in 1931, the Square Four 500cc model was remarkably compact. The original OHC engine is similar to two parallel twins, which share a common crankcase with the two crankshafts geared together at the middle pinions. The overhead cam gear was chain driven and early versions of the Square Four used a hand-change,

four-speed Burman gearbox.

The Square Four grew to 600cc in 1932, giving the motorcycle more power – this increase was intended to be used for a sidecar tug. This Square Four version produced a very smooth ride but the engine proved difficult to tune when looking to improve its performance.

By the late 1930s the 997cc Square Four was introduced with an OHV pushrod, all-iron engine, alongside a similarly engineered 600cc version. The front end still used girder forks with the rear adopting a Frank Anstey's sprung rear suspension system.

After World War II, the Square Four was fitted with an alloy engine, saving around 30lbs in weight. In 1949 the Square Four had a dry weight of around 435lbs and produced 35bhp at 5500rpm. In 1953 the most renowned four-piper Mk2 Square Four, still with Anstey link rear suspension was introduced. Although Ariel began building

prototypes of a Mk3 version in 1954, the model was never put into production. The Mk2 was the last Square Four version to be produced before finally being discontinued in 1959. At this time a new Square Four would have cost £335, but today, collectors and enthusiasts will offer anything up to £4,000 for an original Square Four model.

The Ariel Square Four was one of the most charismatic British bikes ever built after World War II.

Benelli 750

There were six Benelli brothers who began building a wide spectrum of bikes in 1927.

Benelli was established in Pesaro, Italy, in 1911. Originally it was just known as the Benelli Garage, an outfit that repaired cars and motorcycles. By 1920 the company built its first complete engine in-house, a single-cylinder two-stroke 75cc model. A year later, Benelli built its first motorcycle with its very own engine, which had by then become a 98cc model. This was just the beginning of motorcycle construction by the Italian company.

The 750 Sei was the first production six-cylinder motorcycle to be made by Benelli. When Alejandro De Tomaso bought Benelli in 1971 he desperately wanted to create a high-performance luxury sporting motorcycle. The 1970s was the era of the emerging 'superbike' trend, from the Honda 750 and Kawasaki Z1 fours, to the BMW and Ducati twins. As De Tomaso was a fan of the Japanese motorcycle industry, he used the Honda 500 four as a template for his 750 designs.

When the Benelli 750 Sei was launched in 1972 it was essentially a Honda 500 four with two additional cylinders. The Benelli was very similar to the Honda but differed in its use of three Dell'Orto VHB 24mm carburettors, and to minimise engine width the electric start and alternator were mounted behind the cylinders. The engine only produced 71bhp at 8500rpm, but had an extremely smooth ride. After four years of production, Benelli developed the 750 into a 900cc motorcycle, with six-into-two exhausts.

The 750 aspired to combine Japanese-like horsepower with European handling. It was made with quality chassis components including Brembo brakes, Marzocchi suspension and Borrani light alloy wheels. Even though the engine weighed 219kg, the 750 handled very well. The only problem was that it was expensive and not particularly fast, only reaching speeds of around 120mph.

With the 750, De Tomaso tried very hard to overcome many of the problems typically associated with Italian motorcycles of the early 1970s. Not content with unreliable instruments, he fitted the 750 with a proper instrument panel complete with a full set of warning lights. But there was limited appeal for the 750 and being neither truly Italian nor Japanese, the expensive Benelli 750 was taken out of production in 1978.

BMW K1

Although based on the original K100, the K1 was a very different machine. While the general layout was the same, the K1 received a new four-valve cylinder head, which produced an additional 10bhp. It had an improved version of the K100's Bosch fuel injection system, which greatly helped with the engine's overall performance. The K1 produced around 100bhp and yet BMW could have exceeded this limit if it were not for the strict German motoring regulations.

In the United States, emissions regulations pushed the K1's overall power down to 95bhp. The K1 cost almost $13,000 and was rather expensive when compared with its competitors at the time. For example, the Honda CBR600F was just as fast, lighter and cost around $8,500; much less than the K1.

With the market beginning to change in 1993 and the introduction of sports bike models like the Honda Fireblade, the K1 ceased production within the year. A total of 6,921 were sold and, although that figure is regarded by some as disappointing, the K1 helped BMW establish itself as a motorcycle manufacturer and it remains one of their most important machines.

BMW first introduced the radical sport-touring four-cylinder K1 in 1988. During this time BMW was under a barrage of attacks from critics claiming the German manufacturer was having an identity crisis. This break in tradition started in 1982, when BMW launched the inline four-cylinder K100. It featured double-overhead cams, liquid cooling and a Bosch electronic fuel injection system. The K100's 987cc engine was also laid down on its side, making it unlike any other BMW motorcycle.

Throughout the 1970s and early 1980s four-cylinder motorcycles were becoming more and more popular. BMW had squeezed as much performance out of its air-cooled twin engines as they could, and decided the K100 was to be developed as a new generation of motorcycle. Sales were slow at first but soon customers began to warm to these multi-cylinder BMWs. A number of changes were made to the K100 over the next few years but BMW knew it had to get even more power out of the bike.

BMW decided the best way forward was with the release of the K1, which was presented to the public in September 1988.

In order to obtain the maximum performance, BMW engineers decided to wrap the K1 in an all-encompassing aerodynamic fairing.

BMW R32

BMW – manufacturer of German aircraft engines during World War I – was forced to diversify after the Treaty of Versailles in 1919. Initially the company turned to industrial engine design manufacturing before they then began producing motorcycles.

In 1919, BMW had designed and manufactured the flat-twin M2B15 engine for the company Victoria Werke AG of Nuremberg. Initially intended as a portable industrial engine it found its main use in Victoria motorcycles. This engine was also used in the Helios motorcycle built by Bayerische Flugzeug, which later merged into BMW AG. Following the merger, Franz Josef Popp (general director of BMW) asked Max Friz, the design director, for an assessment of the Helios motorcycle. Friz condemned the transverse-crankshaft design so Popp and Friz agreed to redesign the Helios to make a more saleable motorcycle design, resulting in the BMW R32.

Exhibited at the German Motor Show in Berlin in 1923, the R32 proved an instant success, approved by the experts as well as motorcycle consumers. A comment in *Der Motorwagen* magazine at the time read 'And finally, the culmination of the exhibition, the new BMW motorcycle (494cc) with the cylinders arranged transversely. Despite its youth it is a remarkably fast and successful motorcycle.'

The M2B33 486cc engine in the R32 had aluminium alloy cylinders and a light alloy cylinder head. The engine – which formed a single unit with the gearbox – produced 8.5bhp, which gave the motorcycle a top speed of 59mph. The new engine featured a recirculating wet sump oiling system at a time when most motorcycle manufacturers used a total-loss oiling system and BMW continued to use this until 1969. To counter cooling problems found with the Helios, Friz positioned the R32's M2B33 boxer engine with the cylinder heads projecting out on each side to assist with the cooling.

By 1924, BMW was producing the 500cc air-cooled horizontally opposed engine. This feature was used for decades to come, with its driveshaft instead of a chain being used to drive the rear wheel. This was a major innovation and to this day the driveshaft and boxer engine are still used on BMW motorcycles.

The now familiar BMW logo first appeared on the R32.

Brough Superior

In 1919, George Brough set out to begin manufacturing his own motorcycles after parting company with his father WE Brough who had been building Brough machines for a number of years. George Brough wanted to build a much more luxurious machine compared to the reliable and quite pedestrian vehicles that his father made. After George had finished designing his motorcycle he named it the Brough Superior. As well as being more luxurious, it was also much more expensive than any previous Brough vehicles.

George Brough presented his motorcycle at the Olympia Motor Show in 1920 and, after receiving sufficient interest, he began production the following year. This first motorcycle was fitted with an OHV JAP engine; a handful of models used the Swiss Motosacoche V-twin and the Barr and Stroud sleeve-valve engine before the introduction of the SS80 (Super Sports) in 1935 where Brough opted for a more reliable Matchless engine.

Around 400 SS100 models were produced in 1925 with 100 of these being fitted with Matchless engines. In 1938 Brough produced the legendary Golden Dream model, which was an elegant four-cylinder design motorcycle finished in its distinctive gold colour.

Brough also had a number of racing speed record successes. In 1938, during a speed record attempt in Budapest, one motorcycle achieved an astonishing 180mph. However, there was to be no record set as the rider, Eric Fernihough, was sadly killed on the return run after his bike crashed.

With the start of World War II, Brough decided to halt all motorcycle production to assemble aircraft components to help with the ongoing war effort. He continued to do business, building precision engineering tools and Brough Superior parts for many years before his death in 1969.

The Brough Superior has become an extremely sought-after motorcycle by collectors. They have always been rare and expensive machines. During the 1920s, prices for one of these motorcycles ranged from £130 to £180 and only the wealthy were able to afford a Brough Superior. They are valued today at anything from £27,000 to over £2,000,000.

"A skittish motorbike with a touch of blood in it is better than all the riding animals on earth."
Lawrence of Arabia

BSA Gold Star

In 1937, Wal Handley came out of retirement to ride a three-lap race for BSA at Brooklands. This was quite unique in itself, as BSA had not taken part in road racing since the 1921 Isle of Man Clubman's TT where all of the motorcycles that were entered failed to finish. Handley won his race, with a fastest lap speed of 107.5mph and earned himself the Gold Star Pin (awarded for race laps that exceeded 100mph) and with this began the development of the Gold Star motorcycle.

In 1938, the M24 Gold Star was produced, complete with its trademark alloy barrel and cylinder head. The engines were typically built from individually selected parts and bench tested units. The Gold Star was an instant success with customers and was regarded as quite a bargain, selling at £82. It was capable of reaching speeds

of 90mph but lacked the handling to match.

After World War II, BSA launched the ZB32 Gold Star in 1948. Having to fulfil the requirements for the Clubman's TT, over 100 machines were built; 21 of these Gold Stars were entered into the 1949 350cc junior race, which was to be largely dominated by Gold Stars for the next eight years. The 500cc ZB34 Gold Star followed the 350cc model.

The BB series was launched in 1953 and was fitted with a new duplex cradle frame and swinging arm rear suspension. One year later, the CB series was launched with a modified engine to improve performances during road races. This Gold Star series was quickly becoming successful in the Clubman's TT and the engine redesign was used again the following year with the

latest DB series. In 1956, further modifications were made to the cylinder head for the DBD34 Gold Star range.

The very last DBD34 Gold Star was built in 1963. This was not due to a lack of demand, as the motorcycles were regularly winning races but the BSA management had decided they did not want to build any more.

The Gold Star was a model like no other, able to perform in a variety of forms including roadster, touring, endurance racing, scrambling (motocross) trials and international six-day trials.

BSA Bantam

Produced by BSA (Birmingham Small Arms Company) a former shotgun and airgun manufacturer, the BSA Bantam was first produced in 1948. Fitted with a 125cc and then a 175cc engine, the Bantam went on to be produced until 1971. Figures for production vary between a quarter and half a million, though most agree a figure of nearer to half a million units made to be correct.

The original Bantam model was built in 1948 with its three-speed unit construction engine; it came only in the colour mist green and was for export only. This motorcycle was, in fact, a German design and BSA designers converted it to Imperial measurements for manufacture in Birmingham as small motorcycles were becoming more popular in Britain. The Bantam was very economical, giving around 100 miles to a gallon of fuel. The early Bantam's exhausts were 'fish tail' styled though this was later replaced by the more conventional cylindrical silencer. These early Bantam's could average about 50mph and had good brakes for that period.

There was such a great demand for these lightweight motorcycles just after World War II that all production records were broken and it was reported that thousands of people learnt to ride on the Bantam. At that time Bantams were a common sight on British roads and were regularly used when delivering telegrams by the GPO or Royal Mail as they are known today.

One thing BSA had not expected was the use of these motorcycles in competition events. By 1951, the Bantam was designed with an upswept exhaust to replace the earlier 'fish tail' design, with a plunger rear springing giving much more relief to the Bantam's riders. BSA then released both a rigid and plunger motorcycle specifically for competition events.

In 1953 BSA changed the colour from mist green and released a new range of colours. With the Bantam being a popular use for commuting, a dual seat option became available. Modifications were made over the years and by 1968 BSA no longer produced its three-speed Bantam models but instead introduced a four-speed model until the Bantam was finally phased out in 1971.

The first all-over mist green Bantams were sold for £60 plus tax.

BSA Rocket 3

success; however, production delays resulted in it not being introduced until the summer of 1968. For four weeks, the Rocket was labelled as the 'best bike of all time' but once Honda launched the legendary CB750 – with its five speed gearbox, overhead camshaft, electric start and disc brakes – the Rocket 3 was found wanting. Even though it had very good handling and a high top speed, it struggled to impress customers.

The last Rocket 3s were produced in 1973, when BSA shut down their production lines. The company was in a great deal of financial trouble and later that year merged with the Norton Motorcycle Company. Over the course of its seven-year production run, around 28,000 Rocket 3/Tridents were produced. By comparison, around a quarter of a million Honda Goldwing motorcycles were manufactured in the same amount of time.

Testers from Cycle Magazine *called the Rocket 3 "an easy bike to ride fast, its good weight distribution making it easy to fling into corners" in March 1970.*

The BSA Rocket 3 was introduced in the United States during the summer of 1968 in an attempt to see off the increasing waves of successful Japanese motorcycle exports being introduced to the lucrative US market. It is widely considered the first modern superbike and was sold under both the BSA and Triumph – as the Trident – marques respectively.

The BSA Rocket 3 and Triumph Trident were basically badged engineered versions of the same bike, the main difference being the manner and angle of the engine mounting (for further information, please see page 92-93). Whereas the cylinders on the Rocket 3 were canted forward, those on the Trident were vertically mounted.

The three-cylinder engine was designed by Bert Hopwood and was based on Edward Turner's legendary Speed Twin 500cc model of 1937. The aim was to create a truly modern superbike. The Rocket 3 had a 750cc overhead valve engine, which produced 58bhp and had a top speed of 120mph. Had it been released earlier it would have surely been an outstanding

Douglas Dragonfly

The Dragonfly was a British motorcycle designed and built by Douglas motorcycles in Bristol, England and proved to be the last ever motorcycle produced by the company. The Dragonfly was newly styled but based around a previous design but it did not sell well and only 1,600 were produced before the company was taken over.

After World War II, Douglas, like many companies, found itself in financial difficulty. As a result they reduced their output to the 350cc flat-twin models. The flat twin had been widely used by Douglas since 1906 and had a long history of Isle of Man TT racing victories.

The Dragonfly, which was also known as the Dart while in development was launched in 1955. It was originally based on the Mk V Douglas and an earlier 500cc prototype. Aiming to overcome any previous outdated images, designers were bought in from the Reynolds Tube Company to develop a completely new open duplex frame of welded tubing, including a swinging arm with twin Girling dampers with leading link front suspension. The more strengthened and streamlined 348cc engine had a modern coil ignition AC generator with bolt-through cast iron cylinder heads and duralumin pushrods.

When the Dragonfly was launched it was Douglas' last chance to save the company. Although the Dragonfly gained a lot of interest from the outset, the Douglas' stretched finances did not allow the company to exploit this initial demand. As a result the Dragonfly was not produced in very high numbers for another nine months and this proved costly for Douglas.

Production delays were not the

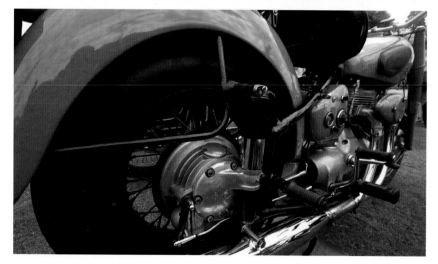

only problem facing the company at that time. The Dragonfly was bigger and heavier than any of its predecessors and no more powerful. It was also rather noisy and acceleration was slow. The Westinghouse Brake and Signal Company bought out Douglas in 1956 and production of all Douglas motorcycles ended in 1957.

Today the Dragonfly has gained a strong following from vintage motorcycle enthusiasts and owners' clubs from around the world.

The London Douglas MCC has become an International Club for Douglas owners and now has over 1,100 members.

The styling of the Dragonfly was radical with the lines of the fuel tank extending forward beyond the steering head and forming an odd looking nacelle.

Ducati 750

The Ducati 750 was a racing motorcycle built by Ducati that won the Imola 200 mile race in 1972. This was a very important win for Ducati as it helped establish the company within the racing scene.

Fabio Taglioni came up with the first designs of the 750 in 1970. The first complete prototype was made by August 1970 and after a number of successful tests it was put into production. Along with the 750, five 500cc V-twins were built to compete in Italian championship and Grand Prix events. Ducati felt that this would demonstrate the bike's performance and gain a great deal of publicity.

Even though the 750 and 500 racers were very similar, the 500 had a much shorter 58mm stroke with its 74mm bore and produced 61bhp at 11000rpm. All Ducati's 500cc GP engines used desmodromic two-valve heads with an 80 degree included valve angle.

In June 1971, the first Ducati 750 GT models came out of the factory, distinguished by their silver frames, metal-flake paint, fibreglass fuel tanks, 30mm Amal carburettors and twin leading shoe rear brakes.

Taglioni experimented with four-valve heads at this time, but was not able to produce any more power than from his two-valve heads, so the two-valve racers were still used. However, Taglioni continued to experiment with four-valve heads right up to 1973.

Mike Hailwood had tested an experimental Seeley frame 750 at Silverstone in August 1971, but he did not think the bike's handling was good enough. Taglioni had also been working on a new frame for the production bike, which was ready and fitted by the Imola 200 in 1972.

Ducati prepared eight 750cc bikes for the Imola 200. The bikes had the new factory frames and 750cc engines that produced 80bhp at 8500rpm. After the race, Ducati received a lot of publicity after two of their bikes finished in first and second place. This win helped inspire the green frame Ducati 750 Super Sports that was launched in 1974.

The Ducati 750 was the first Ducati to bear the L-twin engine configuration.

Ducati 851

The Ducati 851 was first released to the public in 1987. Development had slowed during the years leading up to the 851's release with the continued use of two-valve engines, but new funds enabled a technological move forward which Ducati greatly needed.

Italian manufacturer Cagiva had bought Ducati in 1985 and immediately invested in the development of another V-twin engine but this time with liquid cooling and four-valve desmodromic heads.

The 851 was created to bring Ducati up to speed with the latest engine technology of the time. Before the 851, Ducati had relied on simple air-cooled two-valve

engine designs. Massimo Bordi, one of Ducati's engineers, provided a solution. Bordi had designed a four-valve Desmo in 1973 and, under the guidance of Cagiva, he saw his updated ideas come into production as the Desmoquattro in 1985.

The 851 was largely based on the Pantah motor, but with liquid cooling, fuel injection and desmodromic four-valve heads per cylinder, the cylinder head being designed with the help of UK engine specialists Cosworth. The original prototype was an experimental 748cc four-valve racer which used 750 F1 Pantah crankcases. After more developments, the subsequent 851 road bike had stronger crankcases,

while the heads and valves remained the same, designed to fit above the 88mm bore of a 748cc version.

Between 1987 and 1988 the Ducati 851 Strada was launched and used the signature steel tube trellis frame, Marvic wheels, Brembo brakes and Marzocchi suspension. It was openly criticised for its poor handling, so Ducati changed the front wheel from a 16-inch to a 17-inch wheel, and fitted even better suspension components.

In 1992 the Ducati 888 was released, meaning by this time there were three Ducati superbike models available: the 851 Strada, 888 SP4 and 888 SP4S.

The early Ducati 851 motorcycles suffered from very poor handling characteristics.

Excelsior

Excelsior Motorcycles was a British based company that produced a wide range of machines utilising engines from most major manufacturers. First formed in 1896, they often used Minerva, De Dion, MMC and Condor 850cc single engines. After World War I, Excelsior was taken over by R Walker & Sons and moved from Coventry to Tyseley, Birmingham. Once they were established in their new location they continued to build motorcycles using components produced by Blackburne, JAP and Villiers.

During the interwar years, Excelsior launched a number of successful models, particularly the Manxman, which was perhaps their most famous model. Introduced in 1935 it was available in capacities of 246cc and 349cc. The Manxman took part in its first race at the Isle of Man Lightweight TT in 1935. The following year saw the first appearance of shorter-stroke four-valve cammy racers. They raced again in the 1937 TT in both 250 and 350 capacities but were retired in May 1938.

During World War II, Excelsior produced the Welbike for the army, which was a tiny folding motorcycle designed to be dropped by parachute for use by Special Forces. In the years following the war, racing and luxury machines were put aside in favour of the more inexpensive two-stroke motorcycles. The most famous of these new models was the Talisman twin powered by a 243cc four-speed Villiers engine. However, the company's best-selling motorcycle at that time was the Consort, which had 10,000 units produced annually.

In 1957 Excelsior produced the 98cc Skutabike, and in 1959 released the Monarch, which was essentially a rebadged DKR scooter with an Excelsior 147cc engine. It was later withdrawn in 1960, and production began to slip heavily by 1965 as the company continued to focus on manufacturing car and motorcycle accessories.

Excelsior also produced a number of outboard motors, marine engine gearboxes, and Villiers-powered industrial trolleys. Later the Berkeley SE328 and T60 sports cars also used Excelsior Villiers engines. Both the United States and Germany built motorcycles displaying the Excelsior badge, but these were not related to the British company.

Excelsior Motorcycles first began as bicycle makers, which were originally based in Lower Ford Street, Coventry.

Harley-Davidson Low Rider

In 1977 the first Harley-Davidson Low Rider was introduced at Daytona Bike Week. Also known as the FXS, it was the first of Harley's factory custom models that would later include the Bad Boy, Road King, Fat Boy and the Springer. In addition to its low seat height, the first Low Rider included raised white lettered tyres, drag bars, mag wheels and a two-into-one style slash-cut exhaust. The bike was an instant hit with customers, inspiring a great number of custom models at the time, a trend that continues today.

In the 1980s Harley-Davidson introduced the rubber-mounted FXR chassis to replace the solid-mounted FX line. The Low Rider was to follow the FXRS model. This new model was fitted with dual disk brakes, a pop-up seat and low-rise bars.

Harley-Davidson continued to have a number of problems throughout the 1970s with their Shovelhead engine. In 1984, they introduced an all-alloy Evolution engine that quickly solved almost all of the Shovelhead's past problems. Harley-Davidson models during this time took a lot of flak for being oil-leakers and prone to breakdowns, but their image has stood the test of time and been positive for many years.

The Dyna chassis was introduced in the 1990s and was the first CAD-designed model to be used by Harley-Davidson. The new chassis allowed more engine shake at idle, but less at speed, resulting in vibration-free mirrors during highway cruising. The Dyna chassis had a greater rigidity than its FXR predecessor which allowed for much better handling.

In 2006, Harley-Davidson released a revised line-up of five Dyna models including, Super Glide, Super Glide Custom, Street Bob, Low Rider and Wide Glide. The Low Rider was first introduced in 1977, and it remains a favourite today.

The aptly named Low Rider provides a low centre of gravity with 25.8-inch seat height, stylised low-profile suspension and raked-out forks.

Harley-Davidson Sportster

Manufactured by Harley-Davidson Motor Company, the Sportster, also known as the 'Sportie' was first introduced in 1957. Although Sportster models were produced between 1952 and 1957, these were known as the K models – such as the Sport Solo and K Sport – but were not considered real Sportsters. All Sportster models produced since 1957 have started with the product code 'XL' and this particular model became the longest running production motorcycle in history, with more than 50 years of heritage.

The infrastructure in the United States was changing rapidly during the 1950s, with some 46,000 miles of Super Highways being constructed in 1956 alone. This allowed motorcyclists the freedom to cruise the country in comfort and at speed. All Sportster models were powered by the 45-degree V-twin engine in which both connecting rods of the 'fork and blade' or 'knife and fork' design share a common crankpin. The Sportster also retained the earlier K models' crankcase design, in which the transmission is contained in the same casting as the engine.

The original Sportster, known as the XL Ironhead, was manufactured from 1957 until 1985. It was produced with its 900cc Ironhead overhead-valve engine with cast iron heads, which were eventually replaced by the 1000cc model. Various modifications and new models were introduced in the intervening years before the release of the XR1200 Sportster in 2008.

Harley-Davidson released the XR1200 Sportster in Europe, Africa and the Middle East. This model was not released in the United States until 2009, as Harley-Davidson had to obtain the naming rights for it. The first 750 pre-ordered models came with a

number 1 tag for the front of the bike and the waiting American owners also received a thank you letter signed by Bill Davidson, the great grandson of the co-founder of the Harley-Davidson Company.

The engine has been mounted directly to the frame of each Sportster since 1957.

Honda CB750

The Honda CB750 was built in several model series between 1969 and 2003 and is widely regarded as being the bike that helped to change the face of motorcycling in a number of ways; it set down the design template for the modern superbike with its high-tech specification. The CB750 helped establish the Japanese manufacturer as a new force in motorcycling; with its combination of quality, value and performance it almost single handedly swept aside the flailing British motorcycle industry.

One of the things that created the most impact was the CB750's inline four-cylinder engine. Honda learnt its lesson from the problems faced by the multi-cylinder racers in the 1960s. The inline four-cylinder was smooth, reliable and produced an impressive 67bhp. Buyers were soon won over by the motorcycle's dominance over its competitors. Honda was offering the CB750 with a five-speed gearbox, electric starter and front disc brake, which was a first for any road bike of the time.

The handling could initially only be described as adequate, with the flex-prone steel frame and stiff suspension coming under criticism but Dick Mann proved the CB's sporting potential by winning at Daytona in 1970.

The CB750 had such an impact on the market that, in 1973, Kawasaki delayed and re-engineered its own revolutionary 750cc four-cylinder bike, eventually releasing the Z1 after upping its capacity to 903cc. You don't often get a much finer compliment than that.

In 1976 Honda introduced the CB750A in the United States. It used the same engine as the CB750, but with smaller carburettors producing a lower output of 47bhp. In 1977 the gearing was amended and the exhaust changed but the model was discontinued in 1978 due to increasingly slow sales. The CB750 series was continued in a number of Nighthawk and Hondamatic models from then on.

When Honda introduced the CB750 in June of 1969, the manufacturer dropped the gauntlet that changed the world of motorcycling.

Honda Fireblade

Some say that a misinterpreted translation from French to English for the Japanese word for lightning was the main reason why this bike was known as the Fireblade. Being first produced in 1992, this 893cc bike sold very well and Honda soon found that demand outstripped supply. Producing 124bhp and reaching speeds of 160mph, the Fireblade was proving to be one of the best sports bikes of its time. Over the next few years, the Fireblade had some minor updates and received a redesign to its bodywork.

By 1998 Honda had released a special 50th Anniversary Fireblade model, celebrating Honda's 50 years of producing motorcycles. Honda also released the Fireblade Evolution, which was built to celebrate Honda's 100th win in the Isle of Man TT Races.

Honda had refined the Fireblade during 2000, which now saw it equipped with an all new fuel injected 929cc engine, Usd suspension forks and 17-inch front wheel. A year later, the 954cc Fireblade was released with a much sleeker design; it could produce 149bhp due to better fuel injectors and handling improvements. Weighing 168kg, it was lighter

than the Honda CBR600 and was considered by many as the best-looking Fireblade model of them all.

By 2004, the all-new CBR1000RR Fireblade had a completely new design and boasted a newly developed 998cc in-line four engine. This particular Fireblade had a race developed chassis and weighed 178kg. The engine had a few changes in 2006 and produced 175bhp with a higher rev limit of 12220rpm. It is considered the fastest Fireblade of the time.

Again, in 2008, the CBR1000RR Fireblade was given a new design and featured a sleeker, more compact body. The bike was designed with a twin side exit

exhaust system, which made it much easier to handle.

Throughout 2009 and 2010, the CBR1000RR Fireblade was limited to only four colours in the UK with the United States only having a choice of three. This version stuck with much of the same designs as the 2008 Fireblade and only had a few alterations made to it.

"Make no mistake, the 2003 Fireblade has all the credentials necessary to be a very fast, very scary bike." www. motorbikestoday.com

Honda Goldwing

The Honda Goldwing was first launched as a flat four-cylinder, 999cc. Known as the GL1000 the bike was not immediately accepted by the riding public with Honda only selling 10 percent of the numbers they were anticipating to.

After making some minor changes to the GL1000 design, sales slowly began to increase between 1976 and 1978. The GL1000 received higher handlebars with neoprene grips, a dual contoured saddle and chromed heat shields on the header pipes. Smaller carburettors and shorter valve timing helped increase the performance while in top gear, which was desired by the long distance rider.

The GL1100 was launched in 1980 and was the first bike to have a full touring kit added during production. Customers from all over the world began to buy the bike and Honda's production could not keep up. The GL1100 only lasted until 1982, but Honda was not going to stop there, the next bike was going to be much bigger and better than the last.

The GL1200 was produced in 1984 and then the GL1500 in 1988. After a few years the GL1500 finally got a big change from the original; while only minor changes were made visually there were lots of changes under the bodywork. The suspension was lowered and stiffened yet again helping handling and the seating was lowered by 40mm to help shorter riders. After 10 years in production, the GL1500 was selling nicely and even managed to pull through into the new millennium.

The year 2001 saw the arrival of the GL1800 which was a much

When it comes to touring, there's really only one bike that should ever enter the conversation… the Honda Goldwing.

more modern version of the now dated GL1500. It was rebuilt with a massive 1832cc engine pushing the new design frame around; it was 40lb lighter than the GL1500. The tyres were initially Bridgestone, but after two years they changed back to Dunlop as they always had been.

Honda continue to improve and sell their Goldwing models which are still very popular all over the world, with over a million being produced in the United States alone. As of 2010 all Goldwing models are being produced in Japan.

Indian Scout

The Scout was one of Indian's most important and popular motorcycles. Being produced between 1920 and 1939, the Scout was used by police, motorcycle racers and even by soldiers during World War II.

The Indian Scout was launched in 1920 with a 596cc engine that in 1927 was increased to 745cc. In 1928 the 101 Scout model was introduced, which some consider to be the height of Indian Motorcycle technology. During 1932 and 1941, a number of smaller Scout models were made, known as the Scout Pony, Junior Scout and the Thirty-Fifty.

The Indian Motorcycle Company and Harley-Davidson were the two alternatives for the classic American motorcycle at the beginning of the 20th Century.

Both companies were fierce rivals and, while the Scout was becoming a market bestseller, the Harley-Davidson continually proved to be a very formidable opponent.

The Scout showed its ruggedness and speed when used by racer Burt Munro to set two land speed records between 1962 and 1967. Munro's under-1000cc world speed record set in 1967 still stands today. At the time of his record, 68-year-old New Zealander Munro was riding a 47-year-old, slightly modified Indian Scout motorcycle.

The production of all Indian Scout motorcycle models halted in 1946 after the controlling interest of Indian Motorcycles was sold. Over the coming decades, the company was to have a number of different owners before finally going bankrupt in 1977. After certain legal disputes over the company's ownership were eventually settled in 1998, it resulted in the Indian Motorcycle Company of America (IMCOA) being formed as a conglomerate of nine companies.

Production began again in 1999 and new Scout models were launched between 2001 and 2003. The company was to go bankrupt yet again before reforming in 2006. It relocated to Kings Mountain, North Carolina, but the Indian Scout motorcycle was never made again.

The Scout rivalled the Chief as Indian's most important model.

Kawasaki GPZ900R

The Kawasaki GPZ900R, also known as the Ninja, was a revolutionary new superbike design launched in December 1983. After being developed in secret for over six years, it boasted the world's first 16-valve liquid-cooled four-cylinder motorcycle engine, which proved to be years ahead of its rival manufacturers. Its 908cc engine produced 115bhp, allowing the bike to reach speeds of 151mph which made it the first road bike to exceed the magical 150mph barrier.

Kawasaki had looked into producing its own sub-litre engine before the GPZ900R was designed. Its steel frame, 16-inch front and 18-inch rear wheels, anti-dive forks and air suspension were fairly standard at that time. The engine was positioned lower in the frame which allowed it to reach new levels of performance. Soon after the GPZ900R was launched, it was entered in the Isle of Man Production TT, in which it finished first, second and third at the first time of asking.

New technological advances in later years included water-cooling and 16 valves, which allowed additional power to be gained from the engine. Its new top speed meant it was the fastest production bike of its time and it could complete a standing quarter mile in just 10.5 seconds.

Although the GPZ900R was very performance based, it was extremely smooth to ride in everyday traffic owing a great deal to the new suspension and a crankshaft counter-balancer that made any vibrations minimal. Its aerodynamics combined with good overall engine economy, made comfortable long-distance riding very possible.

The GPZ900R was overtaken by the GPZ1000RX in 1986 but different variations of the GPZ900R were still going strong in the early 2000s – after being sold in Eastern markets including Malaysia – until production ceased in 2003. Most were sold in bright yellow paintwork but otherwise they were almost the same as the model of the early 1990s.

The GPZ900R featured in the 1986 movie Top Gun; *ridden by Tom Cruise it helped transform the bike into a cult icon.*

Kawasaki Z1

Also laying claim to being the world's first superbike, the Kawasaki Z1 was introduced in 1972 by Kawasaki Heavy Industries. Originally designed to be a 750cc four-stroke, four-cylinder machine, Kawasaki went back to the drawing board after Honda shook the motorcycling world in 1969 with the launch of the mighty CB750.

The Z1 was developed under strict secrecy with the project name of 'New York Steak'. The reason for the secrecy was because some years earlier Kawasaki – who manufactured two-stroke motorcycles – decided to produce a 750cc four-stroke sports bike but were beaten when rival company Honda produced the CB750. Following this setback,

the designers were detailed to come up with something much more impressive. The design produced took the motorcycling world by storm. This model, with its 903cc engine and dual overhead cams, created a type of motorcycle that had never been seen before.

In 1973, at Daytona Speedway, Florida, a Z1 set a new world record of 150.8mph for 10 kilometres. It then went on to average 109.6mph for 24 hours, which was yet another world record.

Its handling was not the best; when a *Motor Cycle News* tester rode it at 134mph it began to weave so much that it looked certain to crash but luckily the bike came back under control and received

an enthusiastic write-up. That year *MCN's* readers voted the Z1 the magazine's Motorcycle of the Year. To cash in on the popularity of Z1, all other motorcycle manufacturers had to rethink their designs in order to keep up with the trend.

The Z1 evolved with only minor modifications, colour and styling changes. The same layout was used right up until 1975 when a redesigned model was introduced. The most obvious change during its production was the natural alloy cylinder finish on the 1974 Z10A version before the Z1 was replaced by the Z1000 in 1977.

The lean, mean Z1 will always be remembered as the real thing; the true king of superbikes.

Laverda 750 SFC

Italian company Laverda was once a manufacturer of both high-performance motorcycles and combine harvesters. The agricultural equipment brand is famous for quality, simplicity and efficiency, while their motorcycles gained a reputation for being robust and innovative.

Laverda was mostly recognised as a serious big bike brand with the introduction of the 750 SFC. Many of the first bikes were produced for the American market under the brand 'American Eagle', which were imported to the US from 1968 until 1969. The 750 SFC's introduction quickly halted sales of the recently introduced 650.

The 750 SFC evolved to include disc brakes and cast magnesium wheels. It was launched in 1968 to be ahead of the Japanese competition and featured a new three-cylinder power plant. Four years later, a new 1000 three-cylinder model was put into production. This model shared some of the same features of the 750 SFC such as the engine and the bike's distinctive styling. The 1000cc model had only a few improvements over the 750 SFC but had considerably more power. Along with its size and weight, it quickly won a reputation as a 'Hard Man's bike'.

The 750 models were very much the same as the 650. In 1969, the 750 S and 750 GT were launched, both with an engine and frame that had been reworked with the power increased to 60bhp; just like the agricultural machinery made by the other side of the family business, it was built to be indestructible.

The 750 SFC was developed to win endurance events like the Oss 24 Hours, Barcelona 24 Hours and the Bol D'Or at Le Mans. It began to win a great deal of races and was dominating the international endurance circuit in 1971. This 750 SFC was easily distinguished by its smooth aerodynamic lines, upswept exhaust and characteristic orange paintwork. The model was making a great name for itself and was the flagship product for Laverda, emitting the message of durability and quality.

The SFC 'Series 15,000' was featured as one of the most iconic bikes of the 1970s in New York's 1999 exhibit The Art of the Motorcycle.

Matchless G12

Matchless is one of the oldest British motorcycle manufacturers in the world. A wide range of models were produced under the Matchless name, with the Silver Hawk and the Silver Arrow among the most famous early models. The Colliers bought AJS in 1931, and in 1938 both Matchless and AJS became part of Associated Motorcycles (AMC).

The Matchless G12 was manufactured by AMC at Plumstead, London. This motorcycle, also known as the 'Monarch', was designed by Phil Walker and had a 650cc air-cooled twin engine. Production began in 1958 and ran until late 1966.

By 1959 the De Luxe version was introduced. It was called the G12 De Luxe and was based on the original G12 model having been redesigned and modernised with a new full cradle tubular duplex frame and a new cylinder head. The G12 was described as having an unsurpassed performance and

was capable of reaching 100mph which again proved popular with the American market. Later came an off-road version known as the Matchless G12 CS, but some referred to it as the CS X. This model was aimed at the 'desert racer' rather than as a trials competition machine.

In 1963 the latest Matchless model, the G12 CSR, went on to win the prestigious Thruxton 500 long-distance endurance race. This high-performance motorcycle was fitted with its distinctive two into one 'siamese' exhaust system and upgraded camshafts; however it was particularly prone to leaks and vibration problems. The following year the Matchless G15/45 with an enlarged G12 engine was designed. However, when ridden hard, these motorcycles proved less reliable than the previous 650cc version.

AMC had plans to produce a 750cc desert racer version, but as the company was in financial trouble these plans had to be

abandoned. Had the company been successful in producing this 750cc model it is thought there would have been huge demand from the American market for this powerful desert racer to compete in endurance races.

The G12 was developed specifically to capture the lucrative US market during 1958.

Moto Guzzi Airone

Moto Guzzi is one of Europe's oldest motorcycle manufacturers. Based in Italy, the company is now one of seven brands owned by Piaggio. The company was established in 1921 in Mandello del Lario, the brainchild of three men who met while serving in the Air Corps: Carlo Guzzi, Giovanni Ravelli and Giorgio Parodi. Unfortunately Ravelli was killed in an air accident towards the end of World War I and did not live to see his dream reach fruition.

During the 1930s Moto Guzzi was the biggest and – until the 1960s – the most dominant marque among Italian motorcycle manufacturers. From the beginning, the company traditionally used racing to promote their brand. During the company's successful racing career, Moto Guzzi won 3,329 official races, 14 world championships and 11 times at the Tourist Trophy.

The company has played an important role in Italy's motorcycling manufacture with its prominence in worldwide motorcycle racing and a series of industry innovations, which include the first motorcycle wind tunnel and the first eight-cylinder motorcycle engine.

The Airone 250 was produced from 1939 until 1957 and it was one of the company's most successful motorcycles. The Airone 250 had a pedal-controlled four-speed gearbox and was the most widely used motorcycle in Italy for 15 years. The company continually updated the Airone model making modifications to the suspension and engine for a number of years. By 1949 a new Sports version was introduced which was known as the Airone Sport. This version of the Airone was produced between 1949 and 1957.

After going through quite a bit of financial trouble in the 1960s, Moto Guzzi was bought by Argentinean Alejandro De Tomaso in 1972. Motoring manufacturer Aprilia took control in 2000 before the Piaggio group bought Aprilia in 2004, forming Europe's biggest motorcycle manufacturer. This move has led to a number of new models being produced, which are still around today.

The famous Airone Sport 250 was the most popular medium capacity motorcycle in Italy for almost 15 years.

MTT Y2K

Created by Ted McIntyre of Marine Turbine Technologies Inc, the MTT Turbine Superbike, also known as the Y2K Turbine Superbike, is the world's second wheel-driven motorcycle to be powered by a turbine engine.

In May 1999, the *Café Racer* magazine reported on the MTT Y2K, which was powered by a Rolls-Royce/Allison model 250-turboshaft engine, and showed that it had a recorded top speed of 227mph. The MTT Y2K has features such as smart start ignition, a full colour flat screen digital dash, forward and rear seeking radar detection with laser scrambler. This design secured MTT's place in the turbine vehicle history books. The model was also recognised by the Guinness World Records as both the 'most powerful production motorcycle' and the 'most expensive production motorcycle' in the world with a six-figure price tag.

The MTT Y2K is fitted with a turboshaft engine, which drives the rear wheel via a two-speed gearbox. This was unlike the earlier jet-powered motorcycles that up until 2000 used a massive jet engine providing thrust to push the motorcycle. To avoid the problem of buying kerosene, which is usually needed to power turbine engines, the MTT Y2K engine was made so that it could also run on diesel fuel or even jet fuel.

The American NBC television presenter Jay Leno, a well-known collector of supercars and motorcycles, once described the MTT Y2K as 'smooth', 'amazing' and 'wicked fast' and said of the bike "It's like the hand of God pushing you in the back."

Unlike other contemporary motorcycles, MTT Y2K models from 2001 onwards do not have the 190mph speed-limiting restrictions, which were imposed by Japanese manufacturers.

In 2008, MTT released their latest model, known as the Streetfighter, it was another jet-bike with a more powerful 420bhp engine. The Streetfighter has all the standard features of the MTT Y2K along with a larger swing arm, Pirelli Diablo 240 rear tyre, increased fuel capacity and enhanced cooling system. The Streetfighter is powered by a 320bhp Rolls-Royce/Allison turbine with the option of upgrading to a 420bhp.

Such is the poor fuel economy that a full 32-litre tank would only allow you to ride the MTT Y2K for about 20 minutes.

MV Augusta

The Italian Meccanica Verghera (MV) Company was formed in the small village of Verghera at the end of World War II. The company worked very quickly to release their first model (98cc) in 1945 and it proved to be very popular, doing well in sales and on the racetrack.

During the 1950s, MV Agusta had begun producing a few small capacity roadsters like the Pullman, Turismo Rapido and the Raid. These models were all moderately successful but MV Agusta became a household name due to its racing successes. Between 1958 and 1974, MV Agusta had 17 straight world championship wins in the 500cc class. In the smaller 125cc class, MV Agusta won five championships and two in the 250cc series. There was not a more superior racing name around in the 1970s.

In 1970, MV Agusta introduced the Agusta 750 Sport, which was heavily influenced by its previous racing models. It was an instant success and, although it was expensive, it sold very well. Over the next few years the 750 Sport was updated before the 750S America was introduced for the US market in 1975.

Even with all the company's successes, MV Agusta began to have some financial problems in the early 1970s. The company's founder Count Agusta passed away in 1971 but even under the guidance of his brother Corradino the company still could not break out of its financial dilemma. By 1977, the Agusta family had lost power of the business and this meant that the last motorcycle was to be produced in 1980.

In the 1990s, MV Agusta had re-established itself in the motorcycle market, this time under the ownership of motorcycle company Cagiva. Before long they had produced a new model, the MV Agusta F4 750. This was an attractive model which had almost perfect handling, styling and speed making it very desirable with customers.

Sadly Cagiva ran into their own financial problems and despite all their plans for the new F4 series and developing models, they were unable to continue. New investment soon followed and MV Agusta to this day is still designing new products.

MV Agusta was born with the intention of supplying Italians with a means of transport that was simple and economic following World War II.

Norton Commando

The origins of the Norton Commando can be traced back to the 1940s when the Model 7 Twin was first launched. Designed by Bert Hopwood with a capacity of 497cc, this twin-cylinder design evolved into the 650cc Dominator and 750cc Atlas before being launched as the 750cc Commando in 1967. The main improvement with the Commando over its predecessors was the engine and gearbox were isolated from the frame by special rubber mountings.

Introduced at the Earls Court Motor Show held in September 1967, the Norton Commando was the last twin piston-engined motorcycle produced by the Norton Motorcycle Company. From 1968 until 1972 this motorcycle won the *Motor Cycle News* 'Machine of the Year' competition in the United Kingdom and in the 10 years of its production was popular all over the world.

The frame of the Commando was developed by former Rolls-Royce engineer Dr Stefan Bauer, who was considered revolutionary. Designed around a single 57mm top tube, chief engineer Bernard Hooper used special rubber mountings to isolate the frame from the engine, gearbox and swing arm that had been bolted together. The purpose of this was to eliminate the extreme vibration problems apparent in other models in this range by separating the driver from the engine. Hooper was listed as the inventor on this system's patent document, the system being known as the Isolastic anti-vibration system.

The first production models introduced in April 1968 had frame-bending problems though this was resolved with a new frame being introduced in January 1969. Initially production of this model was complex as different parts were made in different areas of England: the engines being produced in Wolverhampton, the frames in Manchester, while the other components and actual assembly took place at Burrage Grove, Plumstead. However the closure of the Plumstead works in July 1969 meant the assembly line was moved to North Way, Andover.

The owner of Norton Racing Limited, Stuart Garner acquired the Norton brand after several changes of ownership during the latter part of the 20th Century and formed Norton Motorcycles (UK) Limited. This company has produced the new limited edition (200 unit) Commando model, the 961 SE which received favourable comments from *British Motorcycle News* in April 2010.

The 2010 Norton Commando is the first new bike to have this name in more than 30 years.

Norton Dominator

The Dominator was a British motorcycle made by Norton Motorcycles. Designed by Bert Hopwood, it was developed to compete against the successful Triumph Speed Twin.

The Dominator Model 7 had a 497cc iron head engine with a plunger frame and a single twin-spark magneto. Norton used a 360-degree crankshaft layout with a single camshaft at the front of the engine driven by gears and chain. In 1953 the Model 7 had a swinging arm frame fitted, a 19-inch front wheel and a 'pear shaped' silencer. The Model 7 was in production until 1955.

A new featherbed frame was used on the Model 88 Dominator, also known as the De Luxe. It used the same 497cc engine and was developed in 1951 to reach speeds of 90mph. It had better brakes than any other British motorcycle of the time. Originally developed

for export it was sold in the UK from 1953.

The 596cc Model 77 Dominator arrived in 1956 with a swinging arm, single down tube ES2 chassis and a 600cc Dominator 99 engine. By 1960 the featherbed frame was altered so that the top rails were closer together to create what became known as the 'slimline featherbed'. The Norton Dominator 650SS (Super Sports) adopted this new frame which allowed this model to reach speeds of 110mph.

The Norton racing team began using Dominators but they were very much outclassed by the Norton Manx at the time. As a result the Domiracer was produced which had 55bhp. Weighing 35lbs less than the Manx, it proved to be a good quality racer. Dennis Greenfield and Fred Swift both won the 500cc class in the Thruxton 500 in 1960 using this latest model. Tom Phillis lapped the Domiracer at over

100mph, which was a first for a pushrod motor and for any twin in the 1961 Isle of Man TT.

Norton halted the Domiracer project one year later. The Domiracer and factory spares were sold to Paul Dunstall, who continued with development and began producing Norton performance parts, before launching the Norton Dunstall in 1969.

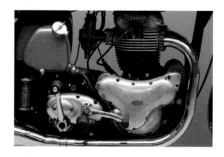

The Dominator design set the pattern for Norton twins for the next 30 years.

Norton Manx

Norton Motorcycles made the Norton Manx, which was also called the Norton 30M, specifically to win the Isle of Man TT. Norton's racing team engineer Joe Craig designed the Manx in 1937 but production was delayed for a year due to certain problems, and the imminent outbreak of World War II. After the war, the Manx re-emerged in time for the 1946 Manx Grand Prix. This model has been described as one of the most effective racing motorcycles ever produced.

The Manx became the tool of choice for professional racers the world over. If the revs could be kept below 7500rpm then a Manx could be raced at the top level each and every week, earning a living for many on the continental circuit. It could be described as the tradesman's white van of the motorcycle-racing world.

In January 1950, the talented McAndless brothers produced for Norton a groundbreaking new design with an all-welded, duplex frame with pivoted rear fork suspension. This was also known as the Featherbed with its low centre of gravity and short wheelbase perfectly suited to the Isle of Man TT course. This particular model recorded a double hat-trick of podium positions at the TT.

In 1954 the Manx engine was redesigned, providing a much shorter stroke of 86mm x 85.6mm giving an improved rev range. Soon after came the Les Archer Norton Manx MX. The British racer Les Archer, frame specialist Ron Hankins and engine turner Ray Petty worked together to develop a Manx motocross motorcycle. This model went on to win the FIM 500cc European Motocross Championship.

The year of 1962 was the last for production of the Norton Manx. However, in 1966, Colin Seeley bought all the tools and remaining parts and sold them to John Tickle three years later who manufactured complete racers called the Manx T5 (500) and also the Manx T3 (350). Unable to compete against the Japanese racers, Tickle sold his stock and rights in the late 1970s to Andy Molnar of Molnar Precisions Limited. The Manx was being produced again, manufactured exactly to the original 1961 specification.

It is still possible to buy a brand-new Manx motorcycle today.

NSU Supermax

The NSU Supermax was first launched in 1956. This motorcycle had the characteristic front springs and dampers on the rear suspension. It differed from its predecessors, the Max Standard and Specialmax models, which only had a single rear spring and damper inside the frame.

The Supermax was a successful model from that period. It proved to be a world reference for many motorcycle manufacturers and even Honda was to take notice of the Supermax. The model's specifically pressed steel frame and fork leading link suspension were both effective and economical to produce. The single-cylinder four-stroke engine offered higher performance levels for its capacity combined with exceptional reliability.

The predecessor of the Supermax was the NSU 251 OSL. This was a successful model from the OSL series, which was built between 1933 and 1940. After World War II, the series underwent only minimal modifications before production began again in 1948.

In 1952 the Max Standard was launched. Producing around 17bhp, it was fitted with iron brake drums and had a small petrol tank capacity of 12 litres. It was widely regarded as very reliable but not a pure sports motorcycle. The Max Standard was originally known as the Max before changing its name.

The Specialmax was produced in 1954 with a larger 'buffalo style' fuel tank containing up to 14 litres. It was fitted with bigger aluminium alloy brake drums, which gave the motorcycle an improved braking performance.

In 1957 NSU produced a special version of the 230 series for the American motocross and endurance events. Called the Scrambler, it was based on the early Geländemax model and was equipped with long front forks, a 21-inch front wheel, shorter mudguard, smaller fuel tank, wider handlebars and a bigger rear light. The engine was the same as in the original Supermax, which produced 18bhp but was also available with a tune-up kit, which increased the engine's performance even more.

In 1963 NSU decided it was not going to produce motorcycles anymore in order for them to concentrate on car manufacture. The last NSU motorcycle was produced in 1967.

The Supermax was fast but docile with excellent handling and road holding.

Panther 100

The Panther Model 100 was a British motorcycle, manufactured by Phelon & Moore and was first introduced in 1932. The Panther name would be used for a variety of models while it was in production between 1932 and 1963. Built in Cleckheaton, Yorkshire, the Panthers had an enviable reputation for their sturdiness and longevity and their long-stroke 600cc engine made them ideal for use with a sidecar. By 1957 the majority of the Panther models sold were equipped with a pivoted fork frame although a few were built with rigid frames. Panther's big four-stroke sidecar motorcycles had a reputation, known as the heavyweights, and their smaller models were referred to as the lightweights.

A 1935 Panther 100 was the machine on which Miss Florence Blenkiron and Miss Teresa Wallach undertook the epic journey from London to Cape Town, crossing the Sahara. It proved to be the first such journey on a motorcycle such as this.

A combination of the collapse of the British motorcycle industry and the increasing number of cheap motorcars brought Panther production to an end. Even so, there are a number of Panther models still in use today after being looked after for many years by their very caring owners.

Phelon & Moore continued to produce some lightweight machines, and the Panther name carried on in the model known as the Red Panther. With its four-stroke single engines and Villiers two-stroke engines, the company was famous for producing the cheapest complete bike in the 1930s at a price just under £30. In 1934, a 250cc Red Panther won the Maudes Trophy, an endurance race.

The line of Panther models ended with the Panther 120 in 1967. For Phelon & Moore this line of Panthers were the most well-known for the company.

While the engine and overall layout stayed essentially the same, the specifications steadily evolved over the bike's production life.

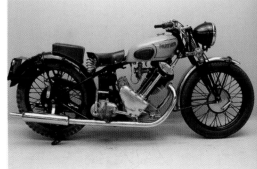

Royal Enfield

Royal Enfield is regarded as a classic motorcycle manufacturer, which still remains popular today. It has a history of production in both England and India, where Royal Enfield models are currently still being made with very little difference in their style or looks.

The first production Royal Enfield was made in 1901. Over the next 30 years, Royal Enfield began to develop a range of new models called the Bullet 250, 350 and 500. Even with an increasing number of models in production, Royal Enfield never managed to match the popularity of companies like Norton, Triumph or BSA.

After World War II, Royal Enfield

Royal Enfield is the oldest motorcycle brand still in production, while the Bullet can lay claim to enjoying the longest motorcycle production run of all time.

financial problems, Royal Enfield was forced to cease production in 1968.

The Royal Enfield brand continued under the name Enfield and the old Royal Enfield factory in Madras was used to restart the brand. The Bullet kept the company alive and they continued producing the popular 350cc model, which sold well in India. Due to export demands, the Bullet was also upgraded with better brakes. The irony is that Enfield was also being exported back to England after halting production in 1968.

Royal Enfield previously had sold motorcycles to India from 1949 and the Bullet was a popular model used by both the Indian police and army, for patrolling the country's border. In 1955, the Redditch Company, which partnered Madras Motors in India, formed 'Enfield India'. The aim was to assemble the 350cc Bullet motorcycle in Madras. Enfield India is still manufacturing vehicles to be sold in India as well as being exported to Europe and America.

decided to redesign the Bullet and have it produced in India to save on labour costs. At this time all motorcycle companies were beginning to build parallel twin engines and Royal Enfield was quick to follow. This eventually led to the 500cc roadster, which later became the Meteor 692cc.

In 1958 the Meteor was upgraded and became known as the Constellation. This new model paved the way for the bigger and more powerful 736cc Interceptor which was produced in 1962. Royal Enfield continued to build and redesign new models over the next few years but, due to a number of

Rudge Ulster

Rudge Whitworth Cycles came into being after a merger of two companies in 1894 and made its name manufacturing bicycles before producing their own Rudge motorcycles between 1911 and 1946. The firm was known for its innovative engine and transmission designs as well as a number of racing successes.

The Ulster was a British motorcycle manufactured from 1929, named after Graham Walker's race win in the Ulster Grand Prix in 1928. Graham was the father of racing commentator Murray Walker.

The same year that Walker was enjoying his triumph in Ulster, Ernie Nott set a world two-hour record at over 100mph on a Rudge motorcycle. He set further speed records in 1929. One year later in 1930, with the help of team boss George Hack, Nott and Walker were racing Rudge 500cc motorcycles at the Isle of Man TT.

A two-valve 250cc was produced in 1935 and the last of the radial four-valve 250cc models were produced in 1936. A 250cc two-valve Sports model was released in 1938, and from early 1939 the Ulster had an RR50 aluminium cylinder head.

When the Great Depression hit in the early 1930s, Rudge – like many other companies – were struggling to stay in business and eventually went into receivership. In 1936, Gramophone Company (who later became HMV and EMI) gave the Rudge Ulster a new lease of life and moved production to Hayes, Middlesex. After a

promising start, development on the Ulster was suddenly halted with the outbreak of World War II. Gramophone Company had to put all their efforts into manufacturing radar and electronic equipment for the war effort.

The Ulster was originally developed as a racing prototype and the production model was essentially a race replica. Over the 10 years of production, a number of modifications were made to the model. Early versions had a four-valve head, with two pairs of valves operating on parallel slopes and could reach a top speed of over 90mph.

The Ulster was advertised as 'probably the fastest 500cc motorcycle in production'.

Scott Flying Squirrel

The Flying Squirrel was a British motorcycle made by the Scott Motorcycle Company. The Squirrel name had been used for Scott motorcycles since 1921 but after the death of the founder Alfred Angas Scott in 1923 these unorthodox two-stroke motorcycles began to become more conventional.

After World War I, production was resumed with the 532cc Standard Tourer and in 1922 Scott began development of its soon to be famous Squirrel model. It was the first sporting model to be offered to the general public after the company had faced severe debt and bankruptcy. The Squirrel was launched at the Earls Court Motorcycle Show in 1926. It was rather expensive, costing nearly twice as much as any other sporting four-stroke motorcycle of the time. Scott employed a unique thermosyphon convection cooling system to lower the temperature on the 596cc two-stroke engine and would paint the bottom of the motor either green or red for racing or road use, respectively.

The Squirrel featured a centrally positioned flywheel, twin inboard main bearings, overhung crankpins and doors to enable ease of access to the engine. The newly redesigned three-speed gearbox, multi-plate clutch and the repositioned electrical generator were all significant improvements.

In 1929 the Squirrel was entered into the Isle of Man Production TT. It finished in a respectable third place and, following this success, Scott Motorcycle Company decided to launch a basic touring model in 1929 for under £70.

However, the company's financial problems continued and in 1931 Scott were unable to enter the Isle of Man TT or the Earls Court Motorcycle Show. Scott lacked the resources to continue producing the Squirrel and by the time World War II began in 1939 production of the motorcycle had completely stopped.

The factory based in Shipley, Yorkshire produced the B2592 air-cooled Aero engines between 1935 and 1938, which were based on the Squirrel's 25bhp producing motorcycle engine. By 1950, however, Birmingham based company Aerco bought the rights to the Scott Motorcycle Company and from 1956 they began producing the Birmingham Scott models until the 1970s.

Scotts were among the first motorcycles to have kick-starts.

Sunbeam S7

The Sunbeam name was taken up by the BSA group in 1943. BSA already had plans for a new motorcycle to be released after World War II and it resulted in a completely new concept in motorcycle design which was entirely different from any pre-war motorcycles.

The first prototype of the Sunbeam S7 was made in 1945 and a great deal of tests were carried out at the factory in Redditch, Worcestershire. In 1946, the S7 was introduced as the flagship model for the BSA range. It was seen as Britain's answer to BMW in the late 1940s and early 1950s. It had a 487cc engine, wedge-shaped combustion chambers and a tandem vertical twin-cylinder overhead camshaft. The S7 could comfortably reach 75mph with its 25bhp powered engine.

The S7's engine is mounted longitudinally in a fully sprung frame. It was fitted with a car type clutch and four-speed gearbox by shaft to an underslung worm drive at the rear wheel. The S7 was described as a 'luxury tourer', it had 16-inch tyres and a cantilever sprung saddle, which – combined with the telescopic front forks and plunger rear suspension – gave the rider a rather comfortable ride.

Two production types were proposed to be built by BSA, the S9 and S10, but they were never put into production. A Sports model was also mooted that had a much higher compression ratio with a different OHC design and could reach speeds of 94mph. It is not certain why this was never put into production but it is rumoured that it was far too powerful for the motorcycle's components to cope with. Yet, others say that it was due to handling problems.

After the Sunbeam production ended, BSA sold the remaining stock of parts to Stewart Engineering. Bob and Chines Stewart were long-time fans of the Sunbeam and in 1963 they decided to form the Sunbeam Owners Fellowship (SOF) to support S7 owners with any problems. A good number of Sunbeam motorcycles survive in perfect working order to this day after many owners followed the advice from SOF.

When the Sunbeam S7 was unveiled to the post-war biking public in 1946, it was one of the most technically advanced motorcycles of its age.

Suzuki Gamma

The Suzuki Gamma, also known as the RG250, was a two-cylinder, 250cc two-stroke motorcycle produced between 1983 and 1987. It was the first mass-produced motorcycle to have a lightweight aluminium frame and racing type aerodynamic fairing. Weighing only 130kg, the RG250 Gamma could produce 45bhp at 8500rpm.

While the other Japanese manufacturers moved in early to begin producing the latest four-stroke machines, Suzuki kept on manufacturing better and larger two-stroke engines. It wasn't until the late 1970s that Suzuki started to make four-stroke engines on a larger scale, despite the fact that one of the first Suzuki models did originally use a four-stroke engine.

The arrival of the RG250 Gamma represented a new phase in Japanese engineering. It was quicker than the Yamaha RD250LC and it was just about as fast as the RD350LC. It had good suspension, which worked very well despite the relatively low weight of the bike and the high build quality had lots of neat touches, which made it nice to look at and very satisfying to drive.

The later Mk2 and Mk3 Gamma models opened up a whole avenue of production racing, which gave many of the other Japanese manufacturers a much needed wakeup call. The Gamma Mk2 was launched in 1985 and had revised front fairings, mudguards and a slightly shorter wheelbase, from 1385mm to 1360mm. The Mk3, also known as the RG500 Gamma, was launched in 1986 and introduced Suzuki's new AEC system (Automatic Exhaust Control). This system gave the bike a much higher power rating of around 49bhp.

By 1987 a very short-lived Mk4 version was created for the Japanese home market. It had larger front discs, thicker tyres and larger diameter front forks. The Gamma was finally replaced by the V-twin engined RGV250 in late 1987.

The Suzuki RG250 Gamma has been described as one of the landmarks of Japanese automotive technology.

Suzuki GS1000

The Suzuki GS1000 was arguably the best of the Japanese litre class motorcycles of the late 1970s.

In 1977, most motorcycle manufacturers were competing against each other by making larger and more powerful motorcycle engines. Kawasaki had released its KZ1000, Yamaha the powerful XS11 and Honda had its GL1000 Goldwing. Suzuki was the last of the Japanese 'big four' to join the exclusive '1000cc club' with the GS1000.

The Suzuki GS1000 was largely based around the successful GS750 model, which was the lightest of the 750s available at the time. Suzuki wanted a simply designed motorcycle that was lightweight and could benefit from solid engineering. The GS1000 was only slightly heavier than the GS750 and was able to produce up to 90bhp.

The GS1000 and GS1000E were launched in February 1978 while the GS1000S – a sports version of the original model – was released soon after. It didn't have the same pneumatic rear suspension as the GS1000 but had an increased rear wheel diameter from 17 to 18 inches. Apparently the German version of the GS1000S did have the pneumatic rear suspension and had a 17-inch rear wheel. Slightly different variations of these bikes were sold in different parts of the world.

The GS series was proving itself on the racetrack too with Wes Cooley winning the AMA Superbike Championship for Suzuki in 1979. The GS1000S was a very fast bike, challenging to be one of the fastest motorcycles in the world. By today's standards, the model was a death machine with its poor stability at high speeds but in 1979 it handled just as well as its competitors. 1980 proved to be the last model year for the GS1000S. The GSX1100S Katana was to then take its place being the fastest Suzuki motorcycle.

A custom version of the GS1000E was launched in 1979 called the GS1000L. It had the same mechanics as the GS1000E but was fitted with higher handlebars, stepped seat, leading axle front fork, a smaller fuel tank and 19-inch wheels. The GS1000L was manufactured between 1979 and 1981. This later GS version was a huge success due to its powerful performance, styling, low weight and good pricing.

Suzuki Katana

The Suzuki Katana was designed in 1979 as a development of Suzuki's popular GS series. As motorcycles should visually appeal to customers, Suzuki set out to change the appearance of their motorcycles. Suzuki teamed up with Hans Muth, Jan Fellstrom and Hans-Georg Kasten of Target Design in an attempt to produce a shockingly different type of motorcycle. After finishing two complete revisions, the final product – the GS1000 Katana – was unveiled at the 1980 Cologne Motor Show.

The first version of the Katana was named after the sword used by the Japanese Samurai. With this in mind, the Katana featured a sharply angled front fairing, clip-on type handlebars, and a 1074cc air-cooled inline four-cylinder engine. Suzuki announced that the Katana would be produced and included in Suzuki's 1981 model line-up. The production model featured a number of small revisions to the original Target design, changing the exhaust layout, lowering seat height and altering the front fairing. When the Katana was launched it would prove to be incredibly popular, despite some people having mixed feelings towards the motorcycle's sharp lines.

Between 1981 and 1983, Suzuki launched the GSX1000S and GS750S Katana models. Both of these models were built with a racing focus in mind and were only produced in small numbers. Although the Katana was intended to be Suzuki's flagship racing motorcycle, the introduction of the GSX-R series in 1985 left the Katana in second place. The Katana series was later dropped down to a sport-touring oriented purpose. Soon after the new GSX-F Katana series was available in a range of 600cc to 1100cc engines but this model strayed away from the original design. The majority of the GSX-F line-up was discontinued in 2004 however the GSX-650F continued to be sold by Suzuki.

The Katana has appeared over the years in a variety of sizes, with early models coming out as 550, 650, 750 and 1100cc versions. 2001 was the last production year for the Katana after a successful lifespan of over 20 years.

Triumph Bonneville

The Triumph Bonneville, also known as the Bonnie, was produced between 1959 and 1983. This model was named after the Bonneville Salt Flats in America where motorcycle companies made attempts to break world speed records.

The Bonneville was produced in Meriden, England and proved very popular in the early 1960s for its performance, which was considered superior to other motorcycles on the market at the time. This 650cc parallel-twin two-cylinder motorcycle was able to reach a top speed of 120mph.

Triumph felt very confident about their new Bonneville model released in 1959. The following statement came from their promotion material when introducing the T120 Bonneville: "The T120 Bonneville offers the highest performance available today from a standard production motorcycle. This is the motorcycle for the really knowledgeable enthusiast who can appreciate and use the power provided."

By 1963 Triumph released an updated Bonneville model, which was stiffer, more compact and included additional bracing at the steering head. Always aware of the performance of their rivals, Triumph later altered the steering angle and improved forks were fitted.

In the early 1970s the T140 Bonneville was introduced. Still sticking with the basic Bonneville design it featured a larger capacity 724cc engine. The engine was then further bored out to 744cc with the addition of front disc brakes. To meet the necessary regulations required by the American market in 1975, the gear change lever was moved from right to left plus a rear disc brake was fitted.

The year of 2001 saw the launch of a completely new model, the Bonneville 790. Initially this new version had a 700cc parallel-

twin engine and then from 2007 onwards all Bonnevilles received the 865cc engine. Throughout 2007, all engines had carburettors but were later switched out for electronic fuel injection systems for all British models in 2008 and to all American models in 2009. However, 'dummy' carburettors were added to 2009 models in an effort to retain the original styling from previous Bonneville models.

Motorcycle stuntman Evel Knievel used a Triumph Bonneville for his attempt at jumping the Caesars Palace fountain in 1968.

Triumph Daytona

The last Daytona model, the T100D, was fitted with a disc front brake but only 14 were built before the closure of the Meriden works in February 1974.

The original Daytona was called the Tiger Daytona T100R 500cc, which was made by Triumph between 1967 and 1974. The name Daytona can be traced back to Buddy Elmore's famous win at the 1966 Daytona 200 race, which was held at the Daytona International Speedway, Daytona Beach, Florida.

After this achievement, Triumph set about producing an updated version of the Tiger Daytona. Chief engineer and designer Doug Hele developed this new model, which was called the Tiger Daytona T100T. Taking influences for the 1966 Daytona 200 race, the T100T was fitted with a new cylinder head and twin Amal Monobloc carburettors. The intake valves were increased and head-valve angles

were reduced to help improve the motorcycle's performance.

Using Edward Turner's original twin-cylinder design, the Daytona was geared towards producing a high power step at 3500rpm. This increase in power limited the engine's flexibility and reduced the life of the valve gear resulting in heavy oil consumption. All this was Triumph's attempt to match and compete with the increasingly advanced designs being produced by Honda.

At the Belgian Grand Prix in 1969, Triumph's factory tester Percy Tait led the world champion Giacomo Agostini for three laps and finished in a respectable second place. Riding his Daytona model, he achieved an average speed of 116mph.

Further upgrades to the Daytona range were made until February 1974 when the closure of the Merlin factory eventually led to the Daytona models being discontinued; of the 4,500 employees, over 3,000 were made redundant; these workers demonstrated against being moved to Small Heath in Birmingham. The Merlin workers co-operative was formed which supplied Triumph 750cc motorcycles to NVT (Norton Villiers Triumph). After NVT collapsed in 1977, the rights for Triumph were bought by the co-operative and became Triumph Motorcycles Limited. Armed with two 750cc models, the Tiger and Bonneville, they started making successful Triumph variants which were sold all over the world.

Triumph Thruxton

The machine on which the Thruxton is based and most credible for the café racers was the Triumph Triton, with a 650cc Bonneville engine.

The design of the Triumph Thruxton was inspired by the café racer bikes of the 1960s where people would centre upon the Ace Café along the North Circular road, London. Bikers would race from one café to the next, in a time before speed limits were properly enforced. This was an era when the most standard of motorcycles were modified to aid performance in racing.

It was launched in 2004 and named after the racing circuit in Hampshire, where Triumph had a famous victory in the Thruxton 500 endurance race of 1962. Riding on the back of this success led to a short production run of 55 T120R Thruxton hand-built racers, which have today become rare and very much sought after.

Engine capacity on release was an air-cooled 865cc which produced 69bhp and 53lb ft of torque. The power enabled a 7,500 red-line zone, giving an eager and crisp delivery, but not quite sport-bike speed. Modified carburettors led the way to a new fuel injection system to meet legislation. Top speed reaches about 110mph achieving a respectable 45-50mpg on a 3.6 gallon tank, giving a range of 180 miles or so. Perfect to use as an everyday, all-purpose bike.

The Thruxton stays faithful to a more modern Bonneville heritage, but enhances with better equipped firmer forks, steeper steering, a longer wheelbase and sharper suspension. The handle bars are set in low forward position and a retro-style period flyscreen was also available. More upright bars were later added, but the riding position still retained a sporty feel. A precise chassis inspires vibration-free confidence and stopping power is provided by twin-piston brake calipers.

Style and quality ooze from this bike to complete a package that captures a spirit from an evocative classic 60s era. Touring accessories and performance bolt-ons can add additional flavour. A bike that is fun to ride, agile and surges forward with ease. Another Triumph British classic.

Triumph Thunderbird

The Triumph Thunderbird, which was also known as the 6T Thunderbird, was first produced in 1949 and continued in its original form until 1966. At this time large powerful bikes were becoming the fashion, and the Thunderbird proved a very popular model. The Thunderbird was launched at Montlhéry near Paris where a team of riders rode their Thunderbirds around a circuit, who between them managed to average a speed of 92mph.

In 1953 all Thunderbirds were typically painted blue, however, the Americans wanted a black model so Triumph complied and for the US version a black model was produced called 'The Blackbird'. Triumph became a household name in America with more being sold there than any other nation.

In 1953, under direction of the South California Timing Association, an attempt was made on a speed record on the Bonneville Salt Flats in Utah. The rider on this Thunderbird changed the sport forever. As was usual in these attempts the riders only wore shoes and bathing trucks in an effort to lower aerodynamic resistance. However after wobbling and coming off the motorcycle while travelling at 130mph he suffered extreme skin injuries resulting in skin grafts taking up to two years to heal. From that accident on riders wore leathers.

Triumph had been bought by BSA in 1951 but ended up as part of Norton Villiers Triumph in 1972 after its parent company had collapsed under the weight of its own debts. It has since had several owners but survives in the 21st Century.

In April 1981 a new model, the TR65 Thunderbird was added to the Triumph range. On introduction this model cost £1,829.82. In 1994 the Thunderbird made a comeback with the Thunderbird 900 and Thunderbird 900 Sport offering upgraded suspension, brakes and wheels while still retaining its classical styling. The last of these was produced in 2004.

In more recent years, during July 2008, Triumph announced a new Thunderbird model was to

Actor Marlon Brando rode his own Thunderbird in the film The Wild One *where sitting astride his motorcycle he portrayed a member of a motorcycle gang.*

be released. Based on the original design, this 1597cc parallel-twin cruiser went on sale in 2009.

Triumph Trident

The Triumph Trident can lay claim to be the first modern superbike and was the last major motorcycle developed by the original Triumph Company.

The Trident was introduced in the United States during the summer of 1968 as Triumph attempted to combat the increasing number of Japanese exports flooding the lucrative US market. Despite the fact that Triumph and BSA had joined forces in 1951, the Trident and BSA's Rocket 3 (for more information see page 20-21), although very similar in specification, did have a number of differing factors. The styling of each motorcycle was unique and the engines were slightly different. The Trident had vertically mounted cylinders, while those on the Rocket 3 were canted forward.

The Trident was considered an extremely good motorcycle on its

arrival and challenged the best in terms of performance. With the introduction of Honda's 750 four, both models were to be put to the test. Both British bikes received minor updates in subsequent years, but the Rocket 3 ceased production in 1973 after BSA hit financial problems. The Trident was redesigned and labelled the T160. This newer version had several additions, the most obvious of which was the adoption of inclined cylinders that allowed for a slightly lower profile. The engine was also fitted with more durable internal hardware and gained an electric starter. To appeal to the American market, the gear lever was moved to the left side of the bike. A 10-inch disc brake was fitted on the front to replace the antiquated drum. In all, 7,000 T160s were built and sold in 1975.

Unfortunately for Triumph, at this time the superbike level

had been raised again, this time by Kawasaki's new Z1 model. Even though the Trident was certainly more improved, it did not measure up to the likes of this new competition. As a result, Triumph faded from the scene after 1976, though the name was revived in 1990 for a more modern, water-cooled, three-cylinder machine to be produced by a new Triumph corporation.

The Trident ultimately succumbed because it was costlier than the more popular Bonneville and slower than the incoming tide of Japanese superbikes.

Velocette KTT

Velocette was a small, family-owned company renowned for the quality of their products. Originally founded by a German immigrant called Johannes Gütgemann, who settled in Birmingham, the company traded under the name Veloce Limited but introduced a range of lightweight Velocette motorcycles in 1913 and the name became popular. Despite the introduction of 350cc OHC bikes in 1925, both the press and public alike continued to designate all models as Velocettes so the firm decided not to fight the trend.

Based on the Velocette KSS, the KTT was developed as a production 350cc racer. This British motorcycle was popularised for having the first positive-stop foot gear change system to be fitted to a motorcycle. This led to significant improvements for racing and it soon began to replace the more difficult hand gear change

levers to become standard on almost all motorcycles from then on.

Percy and Eugene Goodman built the first KTT model in 1924. After a year of development, a KTT driven by Alec Bennett won Velocette their first Isle of Man TT race.

The Velocette KTT continued to be developed in an effort to sort out reliability problems after a number of other retirements. The KTT went on to become the first junior competitor to lap the island course at over 70mph and won several Isle of Man TTs and Grands Prix, which was the amateur version of the TT. Later, the KTT also set a new 350cc world record of 100.4mph at Brooklands.

The 1929 KTT model was modified with a strengthened front fork, originally designed to cope with the very high stresses of sidecar racing. The production racing KTT

went on to become one of the most successful junior TT motorcycles of all time. In 1938, production of the KTT ended and it was to be replaced by the KTT MK VIII after World War II. The Mark VIII was first sold in 1939 and remained in production until 1950 although a few were assembled from spares later, the final one being delivered in 1953. They all had the modern swinging arm rear suspension.

Production of the Velocette KTT Mk VIII continued until 1950 when the Manx Norton took over as the leading TT machine.

Velocette Venom

Originally designed by Charles Udall, the Venom was a single-cylinder motorcycle manufactured by Velocette at Hall Green, Birmingham. Capable of reaching speeds of 100mph, the Venom was first introduced to the public at the Earls Court Motorcycle Show in 1955.

The Venom came fitted with a high compression piston and light alloy chrome plated cylinder head and was painted in black with gold pinstripes. The Venom had the unusual design feature of the clutch between the gearbox and gearbox sprocket, which meant the clutch was less accessible but had the advantage of allowing easier gear changes. The gearbox was also a new Velocette design with a constant mesh close ratio unit that could be maintained relatively easily while still in place.

By 1959 there were two versions of the Venom being steadily produced. These models were the original Venom model and the

Venom Clubman. The Clubman came with a slightly higher compression rate, had rear-set foot-pegs, a reversed gearshift lever and lower handlebars. Although difficult to start at times, Venom Clubman riders found them very fast and easy to maintain.

On 18 March 1961, a standard Venom became the first and only 500cc motorcycle to set the record of travelling over 100mph for 24 hours. This unique Venom that set this world record remains on display at the British National Motorcycle Museum in Birmingham to this day.

In 1965 the Venom Thruxton was launched and was described by many as a true racer. Named after the Thruxton Racing Circuit, it was looking to fill the gap left by the demise of the BSA Gold Star. The Venom Thruxton could reach speeds of 120mph and was more powerful than the original Venom model. A total of 1,108 Venom Thruxtons and 5,721 Venoms were

built but, by 1970, Velocette was forced into liquidation and had to sell off all remaining stock to pay back its creditors.

The Venom Thruxton has become one of the most sought after Velocette motorcycles today.

Velocette Viper

First introduced in October 1955, the Viper was a British motorcycle made by Velocette. Being built using traditional methods and materials, the Viper initially struggled to compete against the more modern machines of that time.

The single-cylinder Viper was designed by Charles Udall and took a great deal of influence from the 349cc Velocette MAC. The Viper's 349cc engine had a bi-metal cylinder with a cast iron liner, high compression piston and a light alloy cylinder head. Using a similar setup to its sister bike, the 500cc Velocette Venom, the Viper had a lot of chrome plating and was available in a choice of black or green paintwork.

Many also considered the Viper as ahead of its time. It was one of the first motorcycles to have a glass fibre enclosure from 1962. However these panels proved unpopular with customers as they extended from the front of the engine, level with the top of the crankcase, to the rear pillion footrests.

In 1960 the Viper Clubman, which was a racing version of the original Viper, was launched. Fitted with TT Amal carburettors, a BTH racing magneto and a close ratio gearbox, with the compression ratio raised to 9.3 to 1. The Clubman had the offending glass fibre enclosure removed, lowered handlebars and a steering damper.

The Velocette development team produced a number of additional Viper models between 1955 and 1968. Twenty-five off-road Vipers, which were known as the Scrambler, were made and exported to the United States to take part in endurance events. Being built to the Viper Clubman design, it had a specially lightened frame. Later in 1962 the Viper Special was introduced. It featured a 3-gallon tank as well as a 100mph speedometer, which was fitted in a modified headlamp housing. The last Viper models were produced in 1968.

The Velocette Viper was one of the most popular 350cc machines available in the 1960s.

Vincent Black Shadow

Produced by Vincent HRD from 1948, the Black Shadow was an entirely hand-built motorcycle. The Black Shadow replaced the earlier Rapide model, due to increasing demand from customers for a more sports based motorcycle. Showing initial influences from the Rapide design, the Black Shadow had been tuned and tested by racer George Brown and Vincent designer Phil Irving. Soon the Black Shadow began to outsell the Rapide and increased in popularity.

One of the main inspirations behind the Black Shadow was soldiers that had served during World War II. The designers wanted to create a motorcycle that could be both operated and maintained by men who had been injured in combat. For example, the clutch could be operated with just two fingers, and maintenance was made much easier than anything previously available.

The engine in the Black Shadow was suspended, instead of being cradled in a set of frame rails, making it a very important part of the bike's structure. The Black Shadow was named accordingly as the entire bike was coloured black, even the engine. Painting the engine made the Black Shadow very different from anything else at that time as most motorcycles were typically covered in polish and shiny chrome.

During the summer of 1955, Phil Vincent announced that Vincent HRD would no longer manufacture motorcycles. The board of Vincent HRD had decided that the company could no longer survive under the continued heavy losses and that production was to be ceased almost immediately. The entire range of Vincent motorcycles was to be discontinued. One week before Christmas 1955, the last Vincent motorcycle was produced. Phil Vincent promised that parts for all of his motorcycles would always be available and to this day, parts are made and sold worldwide by Harper Engineering, who bought Vincent HRD out of receivership.

Just under 1,700 Black Shadows were ever made and are very much sought after by collectors and enthusiasts.

Yamaha FZR1000

When it was first introduced in 1987, the Yamaha FZR1000 was a class-leading sports bike and it brought Yamaha to the forefront of superbike design. The 1987 version had a top speed of over 155mph and by 1989 it was one of the most popular motorcycles of its time. Yamaha continued to improve the bike's performance, notably in 1989 when the engine was enlarged to 1002cc and added an electronically operated exhaust valve, which led to the bike being known as the EXUP.

The FZR1000 was a milestone model as it marked the transition from two-stroke to four-stroke engine in supersport motorcycles. The shift to a four-stroke engine represented a new generation of high-performance motorcycles, which employed Yamaha racing technology from the track. The

first FZR1000 Genesis, presented to the public at the Cologne IFMA Motorcycle Show in Germany on 18 September 1986 continued the success of its supersport predecessors the RD350 and RD500.

The 1989 version of the FZR1000, 'EXUP' was crowned the 'Bike of the Decade' by *Cycle World*. It could reach 0-60mph in 3.9 seconds and had a top speed of over 167mph. Another Yamaha invention, the EXUP system was much like the YPVS system, which was originally in place. The YPVS system was designed to improve two-stroke engine performance by changing exhaust timing in response to changes in engine rpm, the EXUP carried out a similar function but with a four-stroke engine.

The FZR1000 was regarded

by many as the best 1000 model available. From 1989, Yamaha redesigned it making it smaller, lighter and lower and the bike's seat was made wider making it more comfortable for the rider. Since then there have been no major changes to the FZR1000's design, with the exception of a few minor alterations. In its last years of production, it was redesigned to its initial two headlights design and it continued like that until it exited production in 1996.

The original FZR1000 won 'Machine of the Year' awards from numerous magazines across the globe.

Yamaha RD500

With the success in the early 1980s, Kenny Roberts thought back about the Yamaha YZR500 races at Grand Prix and hypothesised that a road going replica of the 500cc racing machine would sell well. He set about designing a new motorbike with the result being the Yamaha RD500, which was launched in 1984.

The RD500's engine used similar technology to the smaller two-stroke RD series but also had elements of the YZR500 engine. It used a 50-degree, twin-crankshaft V4 layout, reaching a maximum speed of 148mph and had a maximum power of 88bhp.

The RD500's frame was made from a mild steel box-section and used a perimeter layout. The rear shock absorber is unusually placed horizontally rather than vertically and was under the engine. The underseat area was occupied by the upper cylinder exhaust chambers, the battery and the YPVS servomotor. The bike weighed 216kg, which included the 22 litres of fuel it could hold. It was a heavier bike compared to the YZR500 but the weight was not all down to its large ignition engine, which only weighed 120lbs. This was achieved by careful and detailed designs.

Normally the engine crank bearings require solid support all the way across, while the gearbox shafts need strong carriage only at their ends. In the RD500 the cranks were put in one case and the gearbox fitted separately into a shell whose ends are the only parts of substance. Each cylinder stud feeds its stress into a heavy boss that carries it directly to the main bearing saddles. The cases were carefully crafted so they were only thick in the places where they needed to keep the liquids and gases where they belonged.

The bike also had an unusually small diameter 16-inch wheel, which was held by 37mm spring and oil damped forks, which featured adjustable anti-dive units. The RD500 used twin-ventilated disc brakes for the front wheel with a single ventilated disc at the rear.

Although short-lived in the UK there were enough RD500s sold to make them a reasonably common sight on the roads at that time. The RG500 stole the thunder out of the RD series in later years as it was imported with an alloy frame which had a slightly better performance over the RD500.

Yamaha V-Max 1200

The Yamaha V-Max 1200 had its first debut at a motorbike dealer show in Las Vegas in October 1984. The bike was targeted for the 1985 season, to be sold initially in the United States. With 145bhp and a V4 1200cc engine, the V-Max had the potential for the most powerful acceleration ever seen before on a road legal production motorcycle. Soon after its introduction in the US, European journalists and customers pushed for the introduction of the V-Max.

The V-Max was known to have a very eccentric style. The designers wanted to place the engine tank low and meeting these restrictions meant it was difficult to fit all the components into place on the machine. Finding that some components just could not fit on, resulted in real problems with the motorcycle's design process. Fortunately this dilemma was solved by the invention of the

V-Boost, which gave unexpected high horsepower and was more compact meaning all the necessary components could fit properly onto the bike.

The V-Boost was a system that opened butterfly valves in the intake manifold between the first and second and between the third and fourth cylinders starting from 5750rpm. The valves opened gradually to match the rising rotational speed signal provided by the ignition system. The V-Boost system added 10 percent to the top power rating of the base engine.

The V-Max was noted for its quick acceleration, however it was also criticised for its poor cornering ability and soft suspension. Despite this though the bike earned the title 'Bike of the Year' from *Cycle Guide* in 1985 and was exported all over the world. The V-Max has been on the market for over 20 years and has only had a few minor modifications

since the 1985 model was launched. The latest model was released in 2008, making it one of the best-selling Japanese motorcycles of all time.

The Honda X-4 was allegedly created in response to the V-Max's overwhelming success, but proved unable to shake its rival's popularity.

Yamaha YZF-R7

The Yamaha YZF-R7 was an approved race motorcycle that had a limited production of only 500 models in 1999. Selling for around £22,000, all 500 of these R7 models were sold, 40 of which came to the UK. It was designed to compete in the World Superbike Championship and Suzuka 8 Hours endurance races. It was specified with Öhlins suspension components, a shortened Deltabox II frame and weight of just slightly over 162kg, which was the minimum for superbike regulations.

The R7 was designed with a racing 'out of the box' intention in mind, which was made obvious in many ways, such as the lack of any passenger provision and by the chassis which was lightweight derived from the geometry of the YZR500 machines of the period. The main frame incorporated an additional layer of aluminium, which helped give it a torsional

stiffness. This was literally twice that of the R1 model and almost 50 percent greater than the YZF-SP racer. As a race bike, the R7 had been designed with 53 percent of its weight over the front wheel, compared to the R1 roadster's 50/50 split.

The R7's roots are clear from the layout of its engine, which combines Yamaha's traditional five-valves-per-cylinder arrangement with the one-piece cylinder-and-crankcase design plus the vertically stacked gearbox that was introduced with the R1. Inside the motor, however, the numerous changes confirmed just how serious Yamaha was about producing a bike good enough to go a step further and win the World Superbike title for the first time. Unlike the old YZF model, the R7 was fuel-injected, with a sophisticated twin-injector system. The combustion dome and intake ports of its cylinder head are

CNC machined, in Formula One race car style. This was to ensure precise dimensions and perfect balance between cylinders. The R7 had greater performance and a greater acceleration speed.

"Just looking at the Yamaha YZF-R7, you know it's going to be good." www.motorcyclenews.com